The Light at the End of the Tunnel.

Santos Omar Medrano Chura

Published by Santos Omar Medrano Chura, 2023.

THE LIGHT AT THE END OF THE TUNNEL.

First edition. November 14, 2023.

Copyright © 2023 Santos Omar Medrano Chura.

ISBN: 979-8223637943

Written by Santos Omar Medrano Chura.

The Light at the End of the Tunnel.
How to Overcome Depression and Regain the Joy of Living.
Author: Santos Omar Medrano Chura

Terms and Conditions

This book is the result of careful and quality work, based on studies of information updated by the editor. However, the information provided may vary due to changes in the Internet. Therefore, we invite you to verify the information and to make your own decisions according to your personal criteria and situation. To make sure you choose what is best for you, we recommend that you consult with a professional before applying anything related to the content of the book. We hope you enjoy this book and that you find it useful.

Index
Introduction.

The light at the end of the tunnel
How to overcome depression and regain the joy of living

Introduction.

Depression is a mental disorder that affects millions of people worldwide. It is characterized by profound sadness, a loss of interest in previously enjoyable activities, low self-estccm, a sense of emptiness, a lack of hope and, in some cases, suicidal thoughts. Depression can have a negative impact on all aspects of life: health, work, relationships, leisure and happiness.

Depression is not a simple matter of mood or character. It is a real illness that has complex and varied causes, which may be biological, psychological or social. Depression is not something to be ashamed of or to blame. Nor is it something that can be overcome by willpower or well-meaning advice alone. Depression requires appropriate treatment and professional and personal support.

The good news is that depression can be overcome. There are effective treatments, both pharmacological and psychological, that can help alleviate symptoms and restore well-being. In addition, there are healthy habits, coping strategies and support resources that can prevent and combat depression. There are also success stories and lessons learned from people who have managed to overcome depression and get back to enjoying life.

This book is intended to provide you with information, guidance and motivation to overcome depression. In it you will find practical tools, useful tips that will help you to better understand your situation, to seek and accept help, to improve your physical and mental health, to manage stress and anxiety, to strengthen your self-esteem and optimism, and to regain the joy of living.

This book is not intended as a substitute for professional medical or psychological care. Nor is it intended to give you magical or miraculous solutions. This book is intended to be a complement and a support for your recovery process. This book is intended to be a friend who accompanies you, listens to you and encourages you on your way to the light at the end of the tunnel.

This book is written in your own words and experiences, based on your personal knowledge and experience of depression. Therefore, this book is unique and original. This book is yours. This book is you.

I hope this book will be of great help to you and that it will help you to overcome depression and improve your quality of life. I invite you to read it with attention, interest and hope. I invite you to put into practice what you learn, to share what you feel and to celebrate what you achieve. I invite you to believe in yourself, in your abilities and in your dreams. I invite you to live fully.

1. Symptoms, causes and types of depression.

- How do I know if I am depressed? The signs you should recognize and not ignore

Depression is an emotional disorder characterized by a persistent low mood that interferes with a person's normal functioning. It is not simply a passing sadness, but a clinical condition that requires professional attention. Some of the most common symptoms of depression are:

Feelings of sadness, tearfulness, emptiness or hopelessness

Outbursts of anger, irritability or frustration

Loss of interest or pleasure in activities once enjoyed

Sleep disturbances, such as insomnia or hypersomnia

Fatigue and lack of energy

Changes in appetite and weight, either from eating more or less than usual

Anxiety, agitation or restlessness

Difficulty in concentrating, thinking, remembering or making decisions

Feelings of guilt, worthlessness or low self-esteem

Negative thoughts about oneself, the future or the past

Suicidal or self-injurious thoughts or attempts

These symptoms can vary in intensity, frequency and duration according to each individual and each depressive episode. To diagnose depression, at least five of these symptoms must be present for at least two weeks and cause significant impairment in the individual's personal, work, social or academic life1.

If you think you may be suffering from depression, it is important that you seek professional help as soon as possible. Depression is a treatable illness and there are different therapeutic options that can help you recover your emotional well-being.

- Why do I feel this way? Biological, psychological and social factors that influence depression.

Depression does not have a single cause, but is the result of the interaction of several biological, psychological and social factors. Some of these factors are:

Biological factors: these refer to chemical and structural alterations in the brain that affect mood. These alterations may be related to the imbalance of neurotransmitters (such as serotonin, noradrenaline and dopamine), hormones (such as cortisol and sex hormones), the immune system (such as inflammation) and genes (such as family inheritance). Some physical illnesses (such as hypothyroidism, cancer or Parkinson's disease) and some medications (such as corticosteroids or contraceptives) can also influence the development of depression.

Psychological factors: these refer to personal characteristics that predispose to or facilitate the onset of depression. These characteristics can be personality (such as neuroticism, perfectionism or low self-esteem), cognitive styles (such as negative thinking, rumination or distortion of reality), emotional styles (such as difficulty in expressing or regulating emotions) and behavioral styles (such as social isolation, lack of physical activity or alcohol or drug use).

Social factors: refer to the environmental circumstances that trigger or maintain depression. These circumstances may include stressful life events (such as bereavement, divorce, unemployment or abuse), conflicting interpersonal relationships (such as lack of social support, domestic violence or workplace bullying) and unfavorable socioeconomic conditions (such as poverty, marginalization or discrimination).

These factors do not act in isolation, but influence and feed back on each other. For example, a person with a perfectionist personality may have more work stress, which may alter their hormonal balance, which in turn may affect their mood and self-esteem, which may hinder their social relationships, which may increase their sense of loneliness and sadness, and so on. Therefore, in order to treat depression, it is necessary to address all the aspects involved in each particular case.

- What type of depression do I have? Differences between major depression, dysthymia and bipolar disorder

Depression is not a single disorder; there are different types of depression depending on its symptoms, severity, duration and course. Some of the most common types of depression are:

Major depression: is the most severe and frequent type of depression. It is characterized by the presence of at least five depressive symptoms for at least two weeks, causing significant impairment in the individual's functioning. Symptoms may be mild, moderate or severe, and may vary with each episode. Major depression may have single or recurrent episodes, and may have special features such as the presence of psychotic symptoms (such as hallucinations or delusions), the presence of melancholic symptoms (such as anhedonia or lack of emotional reactivity), the presence of atypical symptoms (such as increased appetite or sleep), or the presence of seasonal symptoms (such as worsening in winter or spring).

Dysthymia: is a chronic and less severe type of depression than major depression. It is characterized by the presence of at least two symptoms of depression for at least two years, causing persistent but not disabling distress in the individual. Symptoms are usually stable and do not vary much over time. Dysthymia may coexist with episodes of major depression, which is called dual depressive disorder.

Bipolar disorder: is a type of mood disorder characterized by alternating episodes of depression with episodes of mania or hypomania. Mania is an elevated, euphoric or irritable mood that is accompanied by excessive activity, decreased sleep, high self-confidence, verbosity, distractibility and impulsivity. Hypomania is a milder form of mania, which does not cause significant impairment in the individual's functioning. Bipolar disorder can be classified into two types: type I, when there is at least one episode of mania; and type II, when there are only episodes of hypomania.

It is important to know the different types of depression in order to make a proper diagnosis and apply the most effective treatment for each case. If you have doubts about what type of depression you may have, I recommend that you consult with a mental health professional who can evaluate and guide you.

Suggestion:

How do I know if I am depressed? The signs you should recognize and not ignore

Tip 1: Don't minimize or ignore your feelings. Depression is a real illness that affects your physical and mental health. If you feel sadness, emptiness, hopelessness or guilt for more than two weeks, and if these feelings interfere with your daily life, you may be suffering from depression.

Tip 2: Watch your behavioral changes. Depression can affect the way you act and relate to others. If you notice that you have lost interest or pleasure in things you used to enjoy, have difficulty sleeping or eating, feel tired or agitated, isolate yourself or have suicidal thoughts, you may be suffering from depression.

Tip 3: Seek professional help. Depression is a treatable illness and there are different therapeutic options that can help you recover your emotional well-being. Don't be afraid or embarrassed to ask for help. Consult your family doctor or a psychologist who can evaluate you and guide you on the most appropriate treatment for you.

- Why do I feel this way? Biological, psychological and social factors that influence depression.

Tip 4: Identify the factors that may be influencing your depression Depression does not have a single cause, but is the result of the interaction of several biological, psychological and social factors. Some of these factors may include brain chemical imbalance, personality stress, relationships, living conditions, among others. Recognizing these factors can help you better understand your situation and seek solutions.

Tip 5: Don't blame or judge yourself for your depression. Depression is not a weakness, an unwillingness or a bad attitude. Depression is an illness that can affect anyone, regardless of age, gender, culture or socioeconomic status. You are not responsible for having depression, but you are responsible for seeking help and taking care of yourself.

Tip 6: Be compassionate with yourself. Depression can affect your self-esteem and self-confidence. It can make you feel worthless, unworthy or a failure. It's important to treat yourself with respect, caring and understanding. Recognize your strengths, your achievements and your values. Forgive yourself for your mistakes and accept your limitations. Remember that you are a valuable person and worthy of love.

- What type of depression do I have? Differences between major depression, dysthymia and bipolar disorder

Tip 7: Know the different types of depression. Depression is not a single disorder; there are different types of depression depending on its symptoms, severity, duration and course. Some of the most common types are major depression, dysthymia and bipolar disorder. Knowing the different types of depression can help you make a proper diagnosis and apply the most effective treatment for each case.

Tip 8: Don't compare your depression with that of others. Depression is a subjective and personal experience that can vary greatly with each individual and each episode. No two people suffer from the exact same depression or react to it in the same way. Do not feel inferior or superior to anyone else because of your type or degree of depression. Respect your pace and your recovery process.

Tip 9: Keep a positive and hopeful attitude. Depression can make you see everything in black and make you lose faith in the future. However, depression is not an incurable or unsolvable illness. There are effective treatments, healthy habits, support resources and success stories that can help you overcome depression and improve your quality of life.

Don't give up or give in. Have confidence in your resilience and your ability to change.

Tip 10: You are not alone. Depression is a very common illness that affects millions of people around the world. You are not isolated or abandoned. There are many people who love you, support you and accompany you. There are many professionals who guide you, help you and treat you. There are many resources that inform you, motivate you and facilitate you. And there are many books like this one that offer you information, guidance and motivation to overcome depression.

2. Myths and truths about depression

- Depression is not a weakness, a lack of will or a bad attitude.

One of the most widespread and damaging myths about depression is that it is a personal defect, a lack of character or a voluntary choice. This myth implies that people with depression are weak, lazy or negative, and that they could overcome their illness if they tried harder or changed their attitude. This myth generates guilt, shame and stigma in people suffering from depression, and makes it difficult for them to seek help and recover.

The truth is that depression is not a weakness, an unwillingness or a bad attitude. Depression is a real illness that has complex and varied causes, which may be biological, psychological or social. Depression is not something that can be controlled or avoided by just wanting or thinking about it. Depression requires appropriate treatment and professional and personal support.

People with depression are not weak, lazy or negative. On the contrary, they are strong, courageous and resilient people, fighting every day against an illness that robs them of energy, motivation and hope. People with depression deserve respect, understanding and support. People with depression can overcome their illness and regain their emotional well-being.

- Depression does not cure itself, with time or with well-meaning advice.

Another very common and damaging myth about depression is that it is a passing phase, a normal mood or a minor problem. This myth implies that people with depression do not need professional help, but only need time, patience or simple advice to get out of their situation. This myth minimizes the severity and impact of depression, and delays its diagnosis and treatment.

The truth is that depression does not cure itself, with time or well-intentioned advice. Depression is a serious and chronic illness that affects all aspects of life: health, work, relationships, leisure and happiness. Depression is not something that can be overcome just by waiting or listening to phrases like "cheer up", "everything passes" or "don't worry". Depression requires proper treatment and professional and personal support.

People with depression do not need time, patience or simple advice. They need professional help, medication (if necessary), psychological therapy, healthy habits, supportive resources and inspiring testimonials. They need to recognize their problem, seek help and follow treatment. They need to understand their illness, accept it and cope with it.

- Depression is not an incurable, unsolvable or hopeless disease.

The last myth I want to debunk about depression is that it is an incurable, unsolvable or hopeless disease. This myth implies that people with depression are doomed to suffer forever, that there is nothing that can be done to improve their situation and that there is nothing to live for. This myth generates despair, discouragement and suicide in people suffering from depression, and prevents them from seeing the light at the end of the tunnel.

The truth is that depression is not an incurable, unsolvable or hopeless disease. Depression is a treatable and reversible illness that has different therapeutic options that can help alleviate symptoms and restore emotional well-being. Depression is not something that lasts forever and does not determine people's destiny. Depression is solvable and there is hope.

People with depression are not condemned to suffer forever or to give up their dreams. On the contrary, they are people capable of overcoming their illness and improving their quality of life. They are people who have much to contribute and much to enjoy. They are people who have reasons to live and to be happy.

Suggestion:

Depression is not a weakness, a lack of will or a bad attitude.

Tip 1: Don't blame or shame yourself for your depression. Depression is a real illness that has complex and varied causes, which may be biological, psychological or social. Depression is not a personal flaw, a lack of character or a voluntary choice. You are not responsible for having depression, but you are responsible for seeking help and taking care of yourself.

Tip 2: Don't be swayed by prejudices or stigmas about depression. Depression is a very common illness that affects millions of people around the world. You are not alone or isolated. There are many people who understand, support and accompany you. Do not feel inferior or judged because of your depression. You are a valuable person and deserve respect and understanding.

Tip 3: Don't compare yourself or push yourself too hard because of your depression. Depression is an illness that affects your mood, energy, motivation and performance. You can't do things the way you used to or the way you would like to. Respect your pace and your recovery process. Recognize your accomplishments, no matter how small, and celebrate your progress.

- Depression does not cure itself, with time or with well-meaning advice.

Tip 4: Seek professional help as soon as possible. Depression is a serious, chronic illness that requires proper treatment and ongoing monitoring. Do not wait for it to go away on its own or with time. Consult your family doctor or a psychologist who can evaluate you and guide you on the most effective treatment for you.

Tip 5: Follow the treatment prescribed by your mental health professional. Depression can be treated with medication, psychological therapy or a combination of both. Each case is different and requires individualized treatment. Do not stop treatment without consulting your professional, or change the dosage or frequency without his or her consent.

Tip 6: Don't settle for well-meaning but ineffective or counterproductive advice for your depression. There are many people who want to help you, but don't know how to do it or what to tell you. Be grateful for their interest and support, but don't follow their recommendations if they are not based on scientific evidence or if they make you feel worse. Seek reliable and proven information about depression and share it with your loved ones.

- Depression is not an incurable, unsolvable or hopeless disease.

Tip 7: Stay positive and hopeful about your depression. Depression is a treatable and reversible illness that has a solution and can be overcome. Do not lose faith or confidence in yourself and your chances of change. Remember that there are many people who have managed to overcome depression and enjoy life again.

Tip 8: Look for reasons to live and to be happy. Depression can make you see everything in black and make you lose the meaning of life. However, there are many things that are worth living for and for which you can be grateful. Think about your dreams, your goals, your values, your hobbies, your loved ones, your positive experiences, your future projects.

Tip 9: Don't isolate or withdraw into yourself because of your depression. Depression can make you feel alone, misunderstood or rejected. However, you are not alone or isolated. There are many people who love you, support you and are there for you. Seek and accept their help, share with them your feelings and concerns, participate in social or group activities that make you feel good.

Tip 10: Don't give up or give in to your depression. Depression is an illness that has ups and downs, ups and downs, successes and failures. Don't get discouraged or despair if things don't go as expected or if you have relapses. Be patient, persevering and determined. Fight your depression every day and don't let it defeat you.

3. Medical and psychological treatments for depression

- What are my options? Antidepressant drugs, their benefits and side effects

Antidepressant medications are drugs prescribed to treat depression, an illness that affects mood and mental health. Antidepressants act on chemicals in the brain that regulate mood, stress and emotions. There are different types of antidepressants, each with its own characteristics, benefits and side effects. Some of the most common types are:

Selective serotonin reuptake inhibitors (SSRIs): are the most commonly prescribed antidepressants and include fluoxetine, citalopram, sertraline, paroxetine and escitalopram. These drugs increase the level of serotonin, a neurotransmitter related to well-being and happiness. The benefits of SSRIs are that they tend to have fewer side effects than other antidepressants, are effective in treating anxiety and obsessive-compulsive disorder, and have a low risk of overdose. The most common side effects of SSRIs are nausea, vomiting, diarrhea, drowsiness, insomnia, sexual problems, weight gain or loss, and abnormal bleeding1.

Serotonin and norepinephrine reuptake inhibitors (SNRIs): these are similar to SSRIs but also affect the level of norepinephrine, another neurotransmitter involved in mood and energy. The most common are venlafaxine and duloxetine. These drugs are useful for treating depression resistant to other treatments, depression with symptoms of anxiety or chronic pain, and bipolar disorder. The most common side effects of SNRIs are nausea, vomiting, dry mouth, sweating, dizziness, tremors, insomnia, sexual problems and increased blood pressure.

Bupropion: is an atypical antidepressant that acts on dopamine and norepinephrine, two neurotransmitters related to pleasure and motivation. This drug is different from SSRIs or SNRIs because it does not affect serotonin or cause sexual problems. It is also used to treat seasonal affective disorder and to help quit smoking. The most common side effects of bupropion are insomnia, nervousness, agitation, dry mouth, headache and weight loss5.

Older antidepressants: include tricyclics, tetracyclics and monoamine oxidase inhibitors (MAOIs). These drugs act on several neurotransmitters at the same time, giving them greater potency but also more side effects. They are prescribed less often than other antidepressants because they can cause drowsiness, weight gain, hypotension, tachycardia, constipation, blurred vision and difficulty urinating. In addition, MAOIs can cause serious reactions if combined with certain foods or medications. However, they work better for some people than other antidepressants.

The type of antidepressant that is right for you depends on several factors, including your symptoms, the medications or supplements you take, your family history of response to antidepressants, and your personal preferences. It is important to consult with a physician or psychiatrist before starting or changing antidepressant treatment. It is also important to follow the professional's instructions on dosage, duration and monitoring of treatment. Treatment should not be discontinued or changed without your consent.

- How can a professional help me? Psychological therapy, its modalities and objectives

Psychological therapy or psychotherapy is a treatment based on communication between a mental health professional (psychologist or psychotherapist) and a person seeking help to resolve emotional or behavioral problems. Psychological therapy aims to alleviate suffering, improve well-being and promote positive change. There are different modalities and approaches to psychological therapy, each with its own characteristics, benefits and limitations. Some of the most common are:

Cognitive-behavioral therapy (CBT) is one of the most effective and scientifically supported therapies for treating depression. It is based on the idea that thoughts, emotions and behaviors are interrelated and influence each other. CBT helps the person to identify, question and modify the negative or irrational thoughts that generate discomfort, and to replace them with more realistic, objective and adaptive ones. It also teaches the person to cope with situations that cause stress or anxiety, and to develop problem-solving, decision-making, goal-setting and self-esteem skills7. CBT is usually a brief, structured and goal-oriented therapy.

Acceptance and Commitment Therapy (ACT) is a third generation therapy based on the development of psychological flexibility. Psychological flexibility is the ability to contact the present moment, to accept thoughts and feelings without judging or avoiding them, and to act according to personal values. CAT helps the person to accept his or her reality as it is, without fighting or denying it, and to engage in actions that give meaning and purpose to his or her life. CAT is often an experiential, creative and personalized therapy.

Interpersonal psychotherapy (IPT) is a therapy focused on interpersonal relationships that influence a person's mood. IPT helps the person identify and resolve problems with others, such as conflict, loss, role changes or isolation. It also helps them improve their social skills, communication and emotional expression. IPT is usually a brief, present-focused, solution-oriented therapy.

Humanistic therapy is a therapy centered on the person, his or her potential for growth and his or her capacity for choice. Humanistic therapy helps the person to become aware of him/herself, his/her needs, values, feelings and aspirations. It also helps them to develop a positive attitude towards themselves and others, based on respect, trust and responsibility. Humanistic therapy is usually a profound, holistic and individualized therapy.

Psychodynamic therapy is a therapy based on psychoanalysis, which explores the person's unconscious, internal conflicts, childhood traumas and defense mechanisms. Psychodynamic therapy helps the person to understand the root causes of their discomfort, to free themselves from the repressions that prevent them from expressing themselves freely and to integrate the rejected or unknown parts of themselves. Psychodynamic therapy is usually a long, complex and introspective therapy.

The type of psychological therapy appropriate for each person depends on several factors, such as the type and severity of the problem, personality, expectations and personal preferences. It is important to consult with a psychologist or psychotherapist before starting or changing psychological therapy. It is also important to establish a good therapeutic alliance with the professional, based on trust, collaboration and respect.

- What can I do myself? Self-help, its principles and resources

Self-help is a set of strategies that you can apply on your own to improve your mental health and quality of life. Self-help is based on the principles of responsibility, autonomy, learning and change. Self-help is not intended to replace professional care, but to complement and enhance it. Some of the self-help resources you can use are:

Self-help books: these are works written by experts or by people who have overcome depression, which offer you information, guidance and motivation to face your problem. Some examples of self-help books are "El arte de no amargarse la vida" by Rafael Santandreu, "Cómo superar la depresión" by Enrique Rojas or "La luz al final del túnel: cómo vencer la depresión y recuperar la alegría de vivir" by your own author.

Self-help courses or workshops: these are training programs that teach you techniques and skills to manage stress, anxiety, negative thoughts, difficult emotions and problem behaviors. Some examples of self-help courses or workshops are "Learn to control your anxiety" from the National University of Distance Education, "Mindfulness for depression" from the Complutense University of Madrid or "Living without depression" from the Spanish Association of Clinical Psychology and Psychopathology.

Self-help mobile or web applications: are digital tools that allow you to access content, exercises, tips and monitoring to improve your mood and well-being. Some examples of mobile applications or self-help websites are "Moodpath", an app that helps you assess, understand and improve your mental health; "Pacifica", an app that helps you reduce stress and anxiety through cognitive-behavioral techniques; or "Sonrisas", a website that offers resources, testimonials and activities to overcome depression.

Suggestion:

What are my options? Antidepressant drugs, their benefits and side effects

Tip 1: Consult with your doctor or psychiatrist before starting or changing antidepressant treatment. Antidepressants are drugs that are prescribed to treat depression, but they are not all the same and do not have the same effect on everyone. Your mental health professional will be able to evaluate and guide you on the type, dosage, duration and monitoring of treatment that is best for you.

Tip 2: Follow your mental health professional's instructions on the use of antidepressants. Do not stop or change treatment without their consent, or change dosage or frequency without their supervision. Antidepressants can take several weeks to take effect and may cause side effects at the beginning or end of treatment. It is important that you are patient and that you respect the established therapeutic plan.

Tip 3: Learn about the benefits and side effects of antidepressants. Antidepressants act on chemicals in the brain that regulate mood, stress and emotions. Antidepressants can help relieve symptoms of depression, improve your well-being and prevent relapse. However, antidepressants can also cause side effects such as nausea, insomnia, sexual problems, weight gain or loss, among others. These side effects are usually mild and temporary, but if they bother or concern you, consult your mental health professional.

- How can a professional help me? Psychological therapy, its modalities and objectives

Tip 4: Seek professional help as soon as possible. Psychological therapy or psychotherapy is a treatment based on communication between a mental health professional (psychologist or psychotherapist) and a person seeking help to resolve emotional or behavioral problems. Psychological therapy aims to alleviate suffering, improve well-being and promote positive change.

Tip 5: Choose the type of psychological therapy that best suits your needs, preferences and expectations. There are different modalities and approaches to psychological therapy, each with its own characteristics, benefits and limitations. Some of the most common types are cognitive-behavioral therapy, acceptance and commitment therapy, interpersonal psychotherapy, humanistic therapy and psychodynamic therapy. Each type of therapy has its own goals, techniques and duration. Consult with your mental health professional about the options available and the ones best suited for you.

Tip 6: Establish a good therapeutic alliance with your mental health professional. The therapeutic alliance is the bond that is created between therapist and patient, based on trust, collaboration and respect. A good therapeutic alliance is fundamental to the success of treatment, as it facilitates communication, understanding and mutual support. To achieve a good therapeutic alliance it is important to be sincere, open and participative in the therapy sessions.

- What can I do myself? Self-help, its principles and resources

Tip 7: Take responsibility and autonomy in your recovery process. Self-help is a set of strategies that you can apply on your own to improve your mental health and quality of life. Self-help is based on the principles of responsibility, autonomy, learning and change. Self-help is not intended to replace professional care, but to complement and enhance it.

Tip 8: Take advantage of the self-help resources available to you. There are different self-help resources that you can use to inform, guide and motivate you to deal with your depression. Some of these resources are self-help books, self-help courses or workshops, self-help mobile or web applications, self-help groups or self-help forums. These resources provide you with information, tips, exercises, follow-up and testimonials that can help you improve your mood and well-being.

Tip 9: Apply the self-help strategies that are most useful and effective for you. Not all self-help resources are equally valid or appropriate for each person. It is important that you choose the resources that best suit your needs, preferences and goals. It is also important to be consistent and evaluate the results you get with each resource. If a resource does not work for you or makes you feel worse, drop it and look for another one.

Tip 10: Don't isolate or withdraw into yourself because of your depression. Self-help does not mean that you have to do everything alone or that you do not need the help of others. On the contrary, self-help means seeking and accepting the support of people who love you, understand you and are there for you. Share with them your feelings, your worries, your achievements and your difficulties. Participate in social or group activities that make you feel good and bring you benefits.

4. Healthy habits that help you prevent and fight depression

Depression is a mental disorder that affects the way people think, feel and act, causing profound sadness, loss of interest, guilt, irritability, fatigue, difficulty concentrating, sleep and appetite disturbances, and in some cases, suicidal ideation. Depression can have various causes, such as genetic, biological, psychological, social or environmental factors, and can be treated with medication, psychotherapy or a combination of both.

However, in addition to professional treatment, there are a series of healthy habits that can help prevent and combat depression, improving people's physical and emotional well-being. These habits can be grouped into three main areas: taking care of the body, taking care of the mind and taking care of the spirit. Each of these areas and the habits that make them up are described below.

- Take care of your body, take care of your mind: the importance of food, exercise and sleep

The body and mind are closely related, so what we do with our body influences our mood and vice versa. That is why it is essential to take care of our diet, our exercise and our sleep to prevent and combat depression.

Food is the source of energy and nutrients that our body needs to function properly. A balanced, varied and healthy diet helps us to maintain an adequate weight, to prevent physical illnesses and to regulate our mood. Some foods that have been related to the prevention and treatment of depression are those rich in omega-3 (such as oily fish), those rich in tryptophan (such as bananas or dark chocolate), those rich in B vitamins (such as whole grains or legumes) and those rich in antioxidants (such as fruits and vegetables). On the other hand, it is recommended to avoid or reduce the consumption of alcohol, caffeine, refined sugar and processed foods.

Physical exercise is an activity that improves our cardiovascular, muscular and bone health, prevents overweight and obesity, releases endorphins (chemicals that produce pleasure) and reduces stress. Physical exercise also has positive effects on our self-esteem, our confidence and our ability to cope with problems. It is recommended to practice at least 30 minutes of moderate exercise a day, preferably outdoors and in the company of other people.

Sleep is a physiological process that allows us to rest and recover energy, regulate our biological rhythms and consolidate our memory and learning. Adequate sleep helps us to be more alert, focused and creative during the day. Lack or excess of sleep can negatively affect our mood, causing irritability, anxiety or sadness. It is recommended to sleep between 7 and 9 hours a day, following a regular schedule, avoiding long or late naps, avoiding screens before bedtime and creating a comfortable and quiet environment for sleeping.

- Express yourself, connect and enjoy: the importance of communication, relationships and hobbies

Communication is the way we express our thoughts, feelings and needs to others. Communication allows us to share our experiences, resolve conflicts, ask for help and offer support. Effective communication is based on mutual respect, active listening, empathy and assertiveness. Communication helps us prevent and combat depression by avoiding social isolation, relieving emotional discomfort and strengthening our self-esteem.

Relationships are the emotional ties we establish with other people. Relationships provide us with emotional, social and material support. Relationships help us prevent and combat depression by making us feel accompanied, loved and valued. Relationships also provide us with opportunities for learning, fun and personal growth. It is recommended to maintain contact with family and friends, participate in group activities, expand your social circle, and avoid toxic or abusive relationships.

Hobbies are the activities we engage in for pleasure, interest or personal satisfaction. Hobbies help us prevent and combat depression by occupying our free time in a positive way, stimulating our creativity, developing our skills and increasing our self-efficacy. Hobbies also allow us to disconnect from problems, relax and have fun. It is recommended to practice at least one hobby a day, choosing those that we like, motivate and challenge us. We can also take the opportunity to try new things or take up again those we had abandoned.

- Think good, feel good: the importance of self-esteem, optimism and gratitude

Self-esteem is the value we place on ourselves. Self-esteem influences how we feel, how we behave and how we relate to others. High self-esteem makes us feel confident, capable and deserving of love and respect. Low self-esteem makes us feel insecure, incapable and unworthy of love and respect. Self-esteem helps us prevent and combat depression by protecting us from criticism, failure and rejection. It is recommended to improve self-esteem by recognizing our strengths and weaknesses, accepting ourselves as we are, being kind to ourselves and setting realistic goals.

Optimism is the tendency to expect things to turn out well or to see the positive side of situations. Optimism influences how we interpret what happens to us, how we deal with problems and how we project ourselves into the future. Optimism helps us to prevent and combat depression by reducing stress, increasing motivation and generating hope. It is recommended to encourage optimism by looking for the learning or benefit of each experience, avoiding catastrophism or negative generalization, questioning negative thoughts and visualizing positive results.

Gratitude is the feeling of appreciation and recognition for what we have or for what we receive. Gratitude influences how we value what surrounds us, how we express our appreciation and how we contribute to the well-being of others. Gratitude helps us prevent and combat depression by improving our mood, life satisfaction and self-esteem. It is recommended to practice gratitude by writing a gratitude journal, thanking people who help us or make us happy, enjoying the present and being generous with others.

Suggestion:

Take care of your body, take care of your mind: the importance of diet, exercise and sleep

Tip 1: Eat a balanced, varied and healthy diet. Food is the source of energy and nutrients your body and brain need to function properly. A good diet helps you maintain a healthy weight, prevent physical illness and regulate your mood. Include in your diet foods rich in omega-3, tryptophan, B vitamins and antioxidants, which have been linked to the prevention and treatment of depression. Avoid or reduce the consumption of alcohol, caffeine, refined sugar and processed foods, which can negatively affect your mental health.

Tip 2: Practice regular and moderate physical exercise. Physical exercise is an activity that improves your cardiovascular, muscle and bone health, prevents overweight and obesity, releases endorphins and reduces stress. Physical exercise also has positive effects on your self-esteem, confidence and ability to cope with problems. It is recommended to do at least 30 minutes of exercise a day, preferably outdoors and in the company of other people.

Tip 3: Get enough quality sleep. Sleep is a physiological process that allows you to rest and recover energy, regulate your biological rhythms and consolidate your memory and learning. Good sleep helps you be more alert, focused and creative during the day. Too little or too much sleep can affect your mood, causing irritability, anxiety or sadness. It is recommended to sleep between 7 and 9 hours a day, following a regular schedule, avoiding long or late naps, avoiding screens before bedtime and creating a comfortable and quiet environment for sleeping.

- Express yourself, connect and enjoy: the importance of communication, relationships and hobbies

Tip 4: Express yourself with sincerity, respect and assertiveness. Communication is the way you express your thoughts, feelings and needs to others. Communication allows you to share your experiences, resolve conflicts, ask for help and offer support. Good communication is based on mutual respect, active listening, empathy and assertiveness. Communication helps you prevent and combat depression by avoiding social isolation, relieving emotional discomfort and strengthening your self-esteem.

Tip 5: Connect with people who love, understand and support you. Relationships are the emotional ties you establish with other people. Relationships provide you with emotional, social and material support. Relationships help you prevent and fight depression by making you feel accompanied, loved and valued. Relationships also offer you opportunities for learning, fun and personal growth. Keep in touch with family and friends, participate in group activities, expand your social circle, and avoid toxic or abusive relationships.

Tip 6: Enjoy activities that you enjoy, motivate and challenge you. Hobbies are activities that you do for pleasure, interest or personal satisfaction. Hobbies help you prevent and combat depression by occupying your free time in a positive way, stimulating your creativity, developing your skills and increasing your self-efficacy. Hobbies also allow you to disconnect from problems, relax and have fun. Practice at least one hobby a day, choosing those that you enjoy, motivate and challenge you. You can also take the opportunity to try new things or take up hobbies that you have abandoned.

- Think good, feel good: the importance of self-esteem, optimism and gratitude

Tip 7: Value yourself positively, realistically and constructively. Self-esteem is how you value yourself. Self-esteem influences how you feel, how you behave and how you relate to others. Good self-esteem makes you feel confident, capable and worthy of love and respect. Low self-esteem makes you feel insecure, incapable and unworthy of love and respect. Self-esteem helps you prevent and fight depression by protecting you from criticism, failure and rejection. Improve your self-esteem by recognizing your strengths and weaknesses, accepting yourself as you are, being kind to yourself and setting realistic goals.

Tip 8: Hope for the best and prepare for the worst. Optimism is the tendency to expect things to turn out well or to see the positive side of situations. Optimism influences how you interpret what happens to you, how you deal with problems and how you project yourself into the future. Optimism helps you prevent and combat depression by reducing stress, increasing motivation and generating hope. Encourage optimism by looking for the learning or benefit of each experience, avoiding catastrophizing or negative generalization, questioning negative thoughts and visualizing positive outcomes.

Tip 9: Be grateful for what you have and what you receive. Gratitude is the feeling of appreciation and recognition for what you have or what you receive. Gratitude influences how you value your surroundings, how you express your appreciation, and how you contribute to the well-being of others. Gratitude helps you prevent and fight depression by improving your mood, life satisfaction and self-esteem. Practice gratitude by writing a gratitude journal, thanking people who help you or make you happy, enjoying the present and being generous to others.

Tip 10: Be true to yourself and your values. Values are the principles or beliefs that guide the way you live and act. Values help you to give meaning and purpose to your life, to make decisions that are consistent with who you are and what you want, and to feel proud of yourself. Values help you prevent and fight depression by giving you direction, motivation and hope. Identify your values, reflect on them, prioritize them and act accordingly.

5. Coping strategies and relaxation techniques to manage stress and anxiety.

Stress and anxiety are emotional reactions that occur when we perceive a situation as threatening, difficult or unpleasant. Stress and anxiety can negatively affect our physical and mental health, causing symptoms such as muscle tension, palpitations, sweating, shortness of breath, insomnia, irritability, fear, sadness, etc. To prevent and reduce stress and anxiety it is important to learn to use coping strategies and relaxation techniques that help us to better manage our emotions and solve our problems. Three of these strategies and techniques are described below:

- Identify, evaluate and change your negative thoughts: the technique of positive internal dialogue

This technique is based on the fact that our thoughts influence our emotions and behavior. Negative thoughts are those that make us see reality in a distorted, exaggerated or irrational way, generating stress and anxiety. Some examples of negative thoughts are: "Everything goes wrong for me", "I am not capable of doing anything right", "Nobody loves me", "This is horrible and there is no solution", etc. The positive internal dialogue technique consists of identifying these negative thoughts, evaluating their veracity and usefulness, and replacing them with positive thoughts that make us see reality in a more objective, realistic and constructive way. Some examples of positive thoughts are: "I can learn from my mistakes", "I have many qualities and abilities", "There are people who appreciate me and support me", "This is a challenge and I can overcome it", etc. This technique helps us to improve our self-esteem, confidence and motivation.

- Accept, solve and overcome your problems: the problem-solving technique

This technique is based on the fact that stress and anxiety occur when we are faced with situations that present us with difficulties or challenges that we do not know how to solve. The problem-solving technique consists of applying a systematic and rational method to find the best way to deal with these problems. This method consists of the following steps:

1) Identify the problem: clearly define what the problem is, what causes it, what consequences it has and what objective is to be achieved.

2) Generate possible solutions: think of all possible alternatives to solve the problem, without discarding any of them, no matter how absurd they may seem.

3) Evaluate possible solutions: analyze the pros and cons of each alternative, taking into account its feasibility, efficiency, cost and benefit.

4) Choose the best solution: select the alternative that offers the most advantages and the least disadvantages to solve the problem.

5) Implement the solution: put the chosen solution into practice, following a concrete and detailed action plan.

6) Evaluate the solution: check if the solution has worked or not, if the objective has been achieved or not, if there have been side effects or not, etc. This technique helps us to improve our analytical skills, our creativity and our self-efficacy.

- Breathe, relax and release your tensions: Jacobson's progressive relaxation technique.

This technique is based on the fact that stress and anxiety generate a series of physiological changes in our body that cause muscular tension. This tension increases the subjective perception of stress and anxiety. Jacobson's progressive relaxation technique consists of systematically tensing and relaxing the different muscle groups of the body in order to release accumulated tension and reach a state of deep relaxation. This technique consists of the following steps:

1) Adopt a comfortable posture: sit or lie down in a quiet place, with loose clothing and without distractions.

2) Breathe calmly: inhale and exhale slowly through the nose, bringing the air into the abdomen.

3) Tighten and relax the muscles: start with the feet and work your way up through the legs, abdomen, chest, arms, hands, neck, face and scalp. For each muscle group follow the same procedure: contract the muscles for a few seconds, noting the sensation of tension, and then relax them, noting the sensation of relaxation.

4) Maintain relaxation: once the whole body has been walked through, stay for a few minutes in a state of relaxation, enjoying the feeling of calm and well-being. This technique helps us to improve our body awareness, our breathing and our emotional balance.

Suggestion:

Identify, evaluate and change your negative thoughts: the technique of positive internal dialogue

Tip 1: Recognize your negative thoughts. Negative thoughts are those that make you see reality in a distorted, exaggerated or irrational way, generating stress and anxiety. Some examples of negative thoughts are: "Everything goes wrong for me", "I am not capable of doing anything right", "Nobody loves me", "This is horrible and there is no solution", etc. These thoughts are usually automatic, that is, they appear without you noticing them, and repetitive, that is, they repeat over and over again in your mind. To identify your negative thoughts, you can write them down on paper or in an app, or say them out loud.

Tip 2: Question your negative thoughts. Negative thoughts are not facts, but subjective interpretations of reality. Therefore, you can question them and analyze whether they are true or false, whether they are based on evidence or assumptions, whether they help or harm you. To question your negative thoughts, you can ask yourself questions such as: What evidence do I have that this is true? Are there other ways of looking at this situation? What would a friend say to me if I told him or her about this? What would happen if I thought the opposite?

Tip 3: Change your negative thoughts for positive ones. Positive thoughts are those that make you see reality in a more objective, realistic and constructive way, reducing stress and anxiety. Some examples of positive thoughts are: "I can learn from my mistakes", "I have many qualities and abilities", "There are people who appreciate and support me", "This is a challenge and I can overcome it", etc. These thoughts are not false or illusory, but are in line with facts and possibilities. To change your negative thoughts into positive ones, you can use positive affirmations, i.e. short and simple sentences that express what you want to think or feel.

- Accept, solve and overcome your problems: the problem-solving technique

Tip 4: Accept your problems as part of life. Problems are situations that present us with difficulties or challenges that we do not know how to solve. Problems can be of different types, such as personal, family, work, academic, etc. Problems are inevitable and unpredictable, and we cannot control or avoid them. Therefore, it is best to accept them as part of life, without denying or dramatizing them. Accepting problems does not mean resigning or conforming, but recognizing them and assuming them with responsibility.

Tip 5: Solve your problems with a systematic and rational method. The problem-solving technique consists of applying a systematic and rational method to find the best way to deal with problems. This method consists of the following steps: 1) Identify the problem: clearly define what the problem is, what causes it, what consequences it has, and what goal you want to achieve. 2) Generate possible solutions: think of all possible alternatives to solve the problem, without discarding any of them no matter how absurd they may seem. 3) Evaluate the possible solutions: analyze the pros and cons of each alternative, taking into account its feasibility, effectiveness, cost and benefit. 4) Choose the best solution: select the alternative that offers the most advantages and the least disadvantages to solve the problem. 5) Implement the solution: put the chosen solution into practice, following a concrete and detailed action plan. 6) Evaluate the solution: check whether the solution has worked or not, whether the objective has been achieved or not, whether there have been side effects or not, etc.

Tip 6: Overcome your problems with a positive and proactive attitude. Problems do not solve themselves, nor with time, nor with well-meaning advice. Problems are solved with action, that is, with the implementation of the chosen solution. To overcome problems it is important to have a positive and proactive attitude, i.e. to be confident in our abilities, to be motivated by the outcome, to anticipate difficulties and to seek alternative solutions if necessary. It is also important to celebrate achievements, learn from mistakes and ask for help when necessary.

- Breathe, relax and release your tensions: Jacobson's progressive relaxation technique.

Tip 7: Recognize your muscle tensions. Muscle tensions are involuntary contractions of muscles that occur in response to stress and anxiety. Muscle tensions can affect different parts of the body, such as the neck, shoulders, back, abdomen, legs, etc. Muscle tensions can cause pain, stiffness, fatigue and general discomfort. To recognize your muscle tensions, you can pay attention to the sensations you experience in your body, or do a body scan, i.e. mentally scan your body from your feet to your head, noting the most tense and the most relaxed areas.

Tip 8: Relax your muscles with Jacobson's progressive relaxation technique. Jacobson's progressive relaxation technique consists of systematically tensing and relaxing the different muscle groups of the body in order to release accumulated tensions and reach a state of deep relaxation. This technique consists of the following steps: 1) Adopt a comfortable posture: sit or lie down in a quiet place, with loose clothing and without distractions. 2) Breathe calmly: inhale and exhale slowly through the nose, bringing the air into the abdomen. 3) Tighten and relax the muscles: start with the feet and work your way up through the legs, abdomen, chest, arms, hands, neck, face and scalp. For each muscle group follow the same procedure: contract the muscles for a few seconds, noting the sensation of tension, and then relax them, noting the sensation of relaxation.

Tip 9: Maintain relaxation with deep and conscious breathing. Breathing is a vital process that allows us to oxygenate our body and regulate our emotional state. Deep, conscious breathing helps us maintain the relaxation we have achieved with the previous technique by reducing our heart rate, blood pressure and cortisol level (the stress hormone). Deep, conscious breathing consists of breathing through the nose, bringing the air into the abdomen (not the chest), lengthening the exhalation more than the inhalation, and paying attention to the flow of air in and out of the body.

Tip 10: Enjoy relaxation with positive visualization. Visualization is a technique that consists of mentally imagining a scene or situation that produces pleasure, well-being or tranquility. Visualization helps us to enjoy the relaxation that we have achieved with the previous techniques, by activating the same brain areas that are activated when we live that scene or situation in reality. Visualization also helps us to improve our mood, self-esteem and confidence. A positive visualization consists of closing our eyes, imagining a place that we like or relaxes us (such as a beach, a forest, a mountain, etc.), and incorporating all our senses (sight, hearing, smell, touch and taste) to make it more realistic.

6. Support resources and networks for people with depression.

- You are not alone, you are not isolated: the importance of seeking and accepting help

Depression is an illness that affects millions of people around the world, but it is often suffered in silence and in solitude. Depression can cause you to feel misunderstood, rejected, ashamed or guilty, and to isolate yourself from others. However, social isolation only makes depression worse, as it deprives you of the emotional, social and material support you need to recover. Therefore, it is very important that you seek and accept help when you are depressed. Seeking and accepting help does not mean being weak or dependent, but being brave and responsible. Seeking and accepting help implies recognizing that you have a problem, that you cannot solve it alone and that you need the support of other people. Seeking and accepting help allows you to access support resources and support networks that can facilitate your recovery process.

- Who can I turn to? Family, friends and support groups.

Support resources and support networks are people or organizations that can offer you emotional, social or material support when you have depression. Examples of support resources and support networks include the following:

Family members: these are people with whom you share a kinship or affinity bond. Family members can be a source of emotional, social and material support when you are depressed, as they can listen to you, understand you, encourage you, accompany you, help you with daily tasks, etc. However, not all family members are ready or willing to give you the support you need, so it is important that you choose those with whom you feel most comfortable and secure. It is also important that you inform them about your situation, explain what depression is and how it affects you, and let them know how they can help you.

Friends: are the people with whom you maintain a relationship of affection, trust and loyalty. Friends can be a source of emotional, social and material support when you have depression, since they can listen to you, understand you, encourage you, accompany you, entertain you, etc. Friends can also be a source of information and guidance about depression and the resources available to treat it. However, not all friends are able or willing to give you the support you need, so it is important that you choose those with whom you feel most comfortable and safe. It is also important to let them know about your situation, explain what depression is and how it affects you, and let them know how they can help you.

Support groups are groups made up of people who have or have had depression or some other mental illness. Support groups can be a source of emotional and social support when you have depression, as they allow you to share your experiences, feelings and difficulties with people who understand and accept you. Support groups can also be a source of information and guidance about depression and the resources available to treat it. Support groups can be organized by mental health professionals or by volunteers. They can meet in person or online. Examples of organizations that offer depression support groups include: the Anxiety and Depression Association of America, the Alliance for the Support of People with Depression and Bipolar Disorder, Mental Health America, Funidep or ADEP.

- Where can I find information and guidance? Organizations, institutions and websites specialized in depression.

Information and counseling are key resources for understanding what depression is, how it is diagnosed, how it is treated and how it is prevented. Information and counseling are also useful resources for learning about the rights of people with depression, available mental health services, and ways to access them. Examples of resources for information and counseling on depression include the following:

Organizations are non-profit entities dedicated to the promotion, prevention, care and advocacy of mental health. Organizations can provide information and guidance on depression through brochures, magazines, newsletters, campaigns, conferences, workshops, etc. Organizations may also offer other support services, such as counseling, therapy, education, training, etc. Some examples of organizations that offer information and guidance on depression are: the National Institute of Mental Health, the Pan American Health Organization, the World Health Organization, the World Psychiatric Association or the World Federation for Mental Health.

Institutions: these are public or private entities dedicated to research, education or assistance in the field of mental health. Institutions may offer information and guidance on depression through scientific publications, books, articles, reports, guides, etc. Institutions may also offer other support services, such as diagnosis, treatment, rehabilitation, etc. Some examples of institutions that offer information and guidance on depression are: Mayo Clinic, NYU Langone Medical Center, Instituto Nacional de Psiquiatría Ramón de la Fuente Muñiz, Hospital Clínic de Barcelona or the Karolinska Institute.

Websites: are Internet sites that contain information and guidance on depression and other mental health-related topics. Websites can provide information and guidance on depression through text, images, videos, audios, questionnaires, etc. Websites can also offer other support services, such as forums, chats, blogs, podcasts, mobile applications, etc. Some examples of websites that offer information and guidance on depression are: Psychology and Mind, Psychoreview, Help for Depression, Wake Up or TherapyChat.

Suggestion:

You are not alone, you are not isolated: the importance of seeking and accepting help

Tip 1: Recognize that you have a problem and that you need help. Depression is an illness that affects your physical and mental health and requires proper treatment. It is not a weakness, guilt or shame, but a condition that can affect anyone. You cannot fix it on your own, nor can you expect it to pass with time. You need to seek and accept professional and personal help to recover.

Tip 2: Seek professional help as soon as possible. Professional help is provided by doctors, psychologists, psychiatrists and other mental health specialists. These professionals can assess your situation, diagnose your depression, offer you pharmacological or psychotherapeutic treatment, and monitor your progress. Professional help is essential to treat depression effectively and safely.

Tip 3: Accept help from people who care about you. Personal help is provided by family members, friends, colleagues and other people who care about you. These people can offer you emotional, social and material support, listen to you, understand you, encourage you, accompany you, etc. Personal help is very important to feel accompanied, loved and valued.

- Who can I turn to? Family, friends and support groups.

Tip 4: Turn to your closest and most trusted family members. Family members are people with whom you share a kinship or affinity bond. Family members can be a source of emotional, social and material support when you are depressed, as they can listen to you, understand you, encourage you, accompany you, help you with daily tasks, etc. However, not all family members are ready or willing to give you the support you need, so it is important that you choose those with whom you feel most comfortable and secure. It is also important that you inform them about your situation, explain what depression is and how it affects you, and let them know how they can help you.

Tip 5: Turn to your closest and most trusted friends. Friends are the people with whom you maintain a relationship of affection, trust and loyalty. Friends can be a source of emotional, social and material support when you are depressed, as they can listen to you, understand you, encourage you, accompany you, entertain you, etc. Friends can also be a source of information and guidance about depression and the resources available to treat it. However, not all friends are able or willing to provide you with the support you need, so it is important that you choose those with whom you feel most comfortable and safe. It is also important to let them know about your situation, explain what depression is and how it affects you, and let them know how they can help you.

Tip 6: Use depression support groups. Support groups are groups made up of people who have or have had depression or another mental illness. Support groups can be a source of emotional and social support when you have depression, as they allow you to share your experiences, feelings and difficulties with people who understand and accept you. Support groups can also be a source of information and guidance about depression and the resources available to treat it. Support groups can be organized by mental health professionals or by volunteers. They can meet in person or online. Examples of organizations that offer depression support groups include: Funidep, ADEP, Salud Mental España or Depressió Sense Fronteres.

- Where can I find information and guidance? Organizations, institutions and websites specialized in depression.

Tip 7: Seek information and guidance from mental health organizations. Organizations are non-profit entities dedicated to mental health promotion, prevention, care and advocacy. Organizations can provide you with information and guidance about depression through brochures, magazines, newsletters, campaigns, conferences, workshops, etc. Organizations can also offer you other support services, such as counseling, therapy, education, training, etc. Some examples of organizations that offer information and guidance on depression are: the Pan American Health Organization, the World Health Organization, the World Federation for Mental Health, Salud Mental España or Depressió Sense Fronteres.

Tip 8: Seek information and guidance from mental health institutions. Institutions are public or private entities that are dedicated to research, education or assistance in the field of mental health. Institutions can provide you with information and guidance on depression through scientific publications, books, articles, reports, guides, etc. Institutions may also offer you other support services, such as diagnosis, treatment, rehabilitation, etc. Some examples of institutions that offer information and guidance on depression are: the Instituto Nacional de Psiquiatría Ramón de la Fuente Muñiz, the Hospital Clínic de Barcelona, the Karolinska Institute or the WHO Collaborating Centre for Research and Training in Mental Health.

Tip 9: Look for information and guidance on websites that specialize in depression. Websites are Internet sites that contain information and guidance on depression and other mental health-related topics. Websites can offer you information and guidance on depression through texts, images, videos, audios, questionnaires, etc. Websites can also offer you other support services, such as forums, chats, blogs, podcasts, mobile applications, etc. Some examples of websites that offer information and guidance on depression are: Psychology and Mind, Psychoreview, Help for Depression, Wake Up or TherapyChat.

Tip 10: Seek information and guidance from reliable and up-to-date sources. Information and guidance on depression are critical resources for understanding what depression is, how it is diagnosed, how it is treated, and how it is prevented. However, not all information and guidance found on the internet or in other media is reliable or up-to-date. Therefore, it is important that you seek information and guidance from sources that have a scientific or professional basis, are endorsed by official or recognized agencies, are clear and understandable, respect your privacy and confidentiality, and are regularly updated.

7. Success stories and lessons learned from people who overcame depression.

Depression is an illness that can affect anyone, at any time and for any reason. Depression is characterized by profound sadness, loss of interest, guilt, irritability, tiredness, difficulty concentrating, sleep and appetite disturbances, and in some cases, suicidal ideation. Depression can have a variety of causes, including genetic, biological, psychological, social or environmental factors, and can be treated with medication, psychotherapy or a combination of both.

However, depression is not a life sentence, nor is it a condemnation of suffering. Depression can be overcome with the right help, personal effort and the support of others. Many people have managed to get out of depression and regain the joy of living. Their stories are an example of hope, courage and resilience. Three of these stories are described below:

- Ana's case: how she got out of severe depression after a break-up

Ana was a 35-year-old woman who had been in a stable relationship with her partner for 10 years. One day, her partner told her that he wanted to end the relationship because he had fallen in love with someone else. Ana felt devastated, betrayed and abandoned. She went into a state of denial, anger and depression. She stopped going to work, isolated herself from friends and family, neglected herself and began having suicidal thoughts.

Ana went to her family doctor, who diagnosed her with major depression and prescribed antidepressants. However, Ana did not improve with medication. Her doctor recommended that she seek psychological help. Ana was reluctant to go to a psychologist, thinking that it was a waste of time and money, and that no one could understand what was happening to her. However, her doctor insisted that she try.

Ana decided to give therapy a try. She found a psychologist who specialized in cognitive-behavioral therapy, a modality of psychotherapy that is based on changing negative thoughts and behaviors that generate emotional discomfort. Ana started attending weekly sessions with her psychologist.

In therapy, Ana learned to identify, question and modify her negative thoughts about herself, her ex-partner and her future. She also learned to express her emotions appropriately, to accept the reality of her breakup and to forgive her ex-partner and herself. In addition, she learned to set realistic and positive goals for her life, to resume her daily and pleasurable activities, to improve her self-esteem and confidence, and to expand her social circle.

Ana gradually improved with therapy. She stopped having suicidal thoughts, regained interest in her work and hobbies, reconnected with friends and family, took better care of herself physically and mentally, and even met a new person with whom she began a relationship. Ana overcame her depression and felt happy again.

The lessons that Ana learned from her experience were the following:

Depression is an illness that can be treated with professional help.

Psychological therapy is an effective resource for overcoming depression.

Negative thoughts are distortions of reality that can be changed by positive thoughts.

Negative emotions are normal and can be expressed without harming oneself or others.

Acceptance is the first step to change.

Forgiveness is a way of freeing oneself from the past.

Goals are a way of orienting oneself towards the future.

Activities are a way of dealing with the present.

Self-esteem is a way of loving oneself.

Relationships are a way of sharing with others.

- Luis' case: how he overcame chronic depression after losing his job

Luis was a 45-year-old man who had been working as an engineer in a company for 20 years. One day, his company informed him that he was going to be fired for economic reasons. Luis felt frustrated, humiliated and useless. He entered a state of apathy, hopelessness and depression. He stopped looking for work, locked himself in his house, distanced himself from his friends and family, turned to alcohol and tobacco and began to have health problems.

Luis went to his family doctor, who diagnosed him with chronic depression and prescribed antidepressants. However, Luis did not improve with medication. His doctor recommended that he seek psychological help. Luis refused to go to the psychologist, thinking that it was a sign of weakness and that he had no solution to his problem. However, his doctor insisted that he try it.

Luis decided to give therapy a try. He found a psychologist who specialized in acceptance and commitment therapy, a modality of psychotherapy that is based on accepting negative thoughts and emotions without fighting them, and committing to actions that are aligned with personal values. Luis began attending weekly sessions with his psychologist.

In therapy, Luis learned to observe his negative thoughts and emotions without judging or avoiding them, but recognizing them as part of his experience. He also learned to identify his personal values, that is, what gave meaning and purpose to his life, beyond his work. In addition, he learned to set goals consistent with his values and to take action to achieve them, without being driven by fear or guilt. Thus, Luis began to look for work in other sectors, to volunteer in an NGO, to resume his English studies, to practice sports and meditation, and to strengthen his ties with his friends and family.

Luis gradually improved with therapy. He stopped having depressive symptoms, found a new job that he liked and motivated him, improved his physical and mental health, gave up alcohol and tobacco, and even considered starting a family. Luis overcame his depression and felt happy again.

The lessons Luis learned from his experience were the following:

Depression is an illness that can be treated with professional help.

Psychological therapy is an effective resource for overcoming depression.

Negative thoughts and emotions are mental phenomena that can be accepted without resistance.

Personal values are principles or beliefs that guide our way of living and acting.

Goals are specific and measurable objectives that bring us closer to our values.

Actions are concrete and voluntary behaviors that allow us to achieve our goals.

Flexibility is the ability to adapt to changes and circumstances.

Commitment is the willingness to do what needs to be done to live according to our values.

Health is the balance between body and mind.

Happiness is the result of living a full and meaningful life.

- Maria's case: how she overcame postpartum depression thanks to her family and therapist

Maria was a 30-year-old woman who had just had her first child. Maria had wanted to be a mother for a long time and had had a happy and peaceful pregnancy. However, after delivery, Maria began to feel sad, anxious and insecure. She felt no bond with her baby, had no desire to care for him or her, felt guilty for not being a good mother, and was afraid of hurting him or something bad happening to him. Maria went into a state of postpartum depression.

Maria went to her primary care physician, who diagnosed her with postpartum depression and prescribed antidepressants. However, Maria did not improve with medication. Her doctor recommended that she seek psychological help. Maria was reluctant to go to a psychologist, thinking it was an embarrassment and that no one could understand what was happening to her. However, her doctor insisted that she try.

Maria decided to give therapy a try. She found a psychologist who specialized in interpersonal therapy, a form of psychotherapy based on improving relationships with others and with oneself. Maria began attending weekly sessions with her psychologist.

In therapy, Maria learned to identify and express her emotions appropriately, to communicate better with her partner, family and friends, to ask for and accept help when she needed it, to take care of herself and her baby, and to strengthen her bond with her son. She also learned to recognize and combat the negative thoughts she had about her motherhood, her self-esteem and her future. In addition, she learned to value the positive aspects of her life, to enjoy the present and to have hope for the future.

Maria gradually improved with therapy. She stopped having depressive symptoms, began to feel love and joy for her baby, improved her relationship with her partner and others, regained interest in her activities and projects, and even considered having another child. Maria overcame her postpartum depression and felt happy again.

The lessons Maria learned from her experience were the following:

Postpartum depression is an illness that can be treated with professional help.

Psychological therapy is an effective resource for overcoming postpartum depression.

Emotions are part of our human nature and can be managed in a healthy way.

Communication is the basis of interpersonal relationships and can be improved with social skills.

Help is a sign of strength and confidence in others and in oneself.

Self-care is a way to respect and love yourself.

Bonding is an emotional connection that can be created and strengthened with the baby.

Negative thoughts are distortions of reality that can be changed by positive thoughts.

Positive aspects are the good things we have in our life that we can appreciate and be grateful for.

Happiness is the result of living a full and satisfying life.

Suggestion:

Ana's case: how she got out of severe depression after a break-up

Tip 1: Recognize that you have depression and that you need help. Depression is an illness that affects your physical and mental health and requires proper treatment. It is not a weakness, guilt or shame, but a condition that can affect anyone. You cannot fix it on your own, nor can you expect it to pass with time. You need to seek and accept professional and personal help to recover.

Tip 2: Seek professional help as soon as possible. Professional help is provided by doctors, psychologists, psychiatrists and other mental health specialists. These professionals can assess your situation, diagnose your depression, offer you pharmacological or psychotherapeutic treatment, and monitor your progress. Professional help is essential to treat depression effectively and safely.

Tip 3: Accept help from people who care about you. Personal help is provided by family members, friends, colleagues and other people who care about you. These people can offer you emotional, social and material support, listen to you, understand you, encourage you, accompany you, etc. Personal help is very important to feel accompanied, loved and valued.

Tip 4: Change your negative thoughts for positive ones. Negative thoughts are those that make you see reality in a distorted, exaggerated or irrational way, generating stress and anxiety. Some examples of negative thoughts are: "Everything goes wrong for me", "I am not capable of doing anything right", "Nobody loves me", "This is horrible and has no solution", etc. These thoughts are usually automatic, that is, they appear without you realizing it, and repetitive, that is, they repeat over and over again in your mind. To change your negative thoughts for positive ones, you can use the technique of positive internal dialogue, which consists of identifying these negative thoughts, evaluating their veracity and usefulness, and replacing them with positive thoughts that make you see reality in a more objective, realistic and constructive way. Some examples of positive thoughts are: "I can learn from my mistakes", "I have many qualities and abilities", "There are people who appreciate and support me", "This is a challenge and I can overcome it", etc.

Tip 5: Express your emotions appropriately. Emotions are psychophysiological reactions to certain stimuli or situations. Emotions can be positive or negative, depending on the degree of pleasure or displeasure they generate. Some negative emotions that are usually associated with depression are: sadness, anger, guilt, fear, anxiety, etc. These emotions are normal and natural, but can be harmful if repressed or expressed inappropriately. To express your emotions appropriately, you can use the technique of emotional venting, which consists of releasing your emotions through words or actions that do not harm you or others. Some forms of emotional venting are: talking to someone you trust, writing a diary or letter, crying or shouting in a private place, doing physical exercise or an artistic activity, etc.

Tip 6: Accept the reality of your breakup and forgive your ex-partner and yourself. Love breakup is a painful situation involving the loss of a person with whom you have shared an intimate and meaningful relationship. Love breakup can bring about feelings of sadness, anger, guilt, fear, loneliness, etc. To overcome a breakup, it is necessary to accept the reality of what has happened, without denying it or dramatizing it. Accepting reality implies recognizing that the relationship is over, that you cannot go back, and that you have to move on. To accept reality, you can use the technique of radical acceptance, which consists of assuming what has happened without judging it or resisting it, but seeing it as an inevitable and neutral fact. In addition to accepting reality, it is important to forgive your ex-partner and yourself for what has happened.

Forgiving does not mean forgetting or justifying, but freeing yourself from resentment and resentment. To forgive, you can use the technique of compassionate forgiveness, which consists of understanding the reasons and emotions of your ex-partner and yourself, without blaming or victimizing anyone, but recognizing that we are all human and make mistakes.

Tip 7: Set realistic and positive goals for your life. Goals are objectives that we set out to achieve within a certain period of time. Goals help us to orient our life towards what we want and motivate us to act to achieve it. However, not all goals are appropriate or beneficial for us. For a goal to be effective and healthy, it must meet the following characteristics: be specific, measurable, achievable, relevant and time-bound. For example, an appropriate goal would be: "I want to find a job that I like and that will allow me to make a decent living in the next six months". An inappropriate goal would be: "I want to be rich and famous someday". In addition to meeting these characteristics, goals should be positive, that is, they should be formulated in terms of what you want to achieve and not what you want to avoid. For example, a positive goal would be: "I want to be happy and have a fulfilling life". A negative goal would be: "I don't want to be sad or have an empty life".

Tip 8: Engage in pleasurable daily activities. Activities are actions we perform in our daily lives that allow us to take care of our basic needs, our obligations and our interests. Activities can be daily or pleasurable. Everyday activities are those that we have to do out of necessity or responsibility, such as eating, sleeping, grooming, working, studying, etc. Pleasurable activities are those that we do for pleasure or fun, such as reading, watching a movie, listening to music, practicing a hobby, etc. Both types of activities are important for our physical and mental well-being. Everyday activities help us to maintain a routine and order in our lives, to feel useful and productive, and to satisfy our basic needs. Pleasurable activities help us to enjoy the present, to feel happy and fulfilled, and to develop our capabilities and potential.

Tip 9: Improve your self-esteem and confidence. Self-esteem is the set of perceptions, evaluations and feelings we have about ourselves. Self-esteem influences how we see ourselves, how we treat ourselves and how we relate to others. Self-esteem can be high or low. High self-esteem implies having a positive self-image, valuing and loving oneself as one is, respecting and caring for oneself, trusting one's own abilities and opinions, etc. Low self-esteem implies having a negative self-image, devaluing and despising oneself as one is, disrespecting and neglecting oneself, doubting one's own abilities and opinions, etc. To improve self-esteem, the technique of positive reinforcement can be used, which consists of recognizing and rewarding one's own achievements, qualities and virtues, without comparing oneself or competing with others.

Tip 10: Strengthen your bonds with others. Attachments are the affective connections we establish with other people. Attachments help us to feel accompanied, loved and supported, to share our experiences, feelings and needs, to learn from others and to grow as people. Bonds can be of different types, such as family, friendships, romantic, professional, etc. To strengthen your bonds with others, you can use the technique of effective communication, which consists of expressing your ideas, opinions and emotions in a clear, respectful and assertive way, actively listening to others, showing interest and empathy for what they say and feel, giving and receiving constructive feedback, resolving conflicts peacefully, etc.

Luis' case: how he overcame chronic depression after losing his job

Tip 1: Recognize that you have depression and that you need help. Depression is an illness that affects your physical and mental health and requires proper treatment. It is not a weakness, guilt or shame, but a condition that can affect anyone. You cannot fix it on your own, nor can you expect it to pass with time. You need to seek and accept professional and personal help to recover.

Tip 2: Seek professional help as soon as possible. Professional help is provided by doctors, psychologists, psychiatrists and other mental health specialists. These professionals can assess your situation, diagnose your depression, offer you pharmacological or psychotherapeutic treatment, and monitor your progress. Professional help is essential to treat depression effectively and safely.

Tip 3: Accept help from people who care about you. Personal help is provided by family members, friends, colleagues and other people who care about you. These people can offer you emotional, social and material support, listen to you, understand you, encourage you, accompany you, etc. Personal help is very important to feel accompanied, loved and valued.

Tip 4: Accept your negative thoughts and emotions without fighting them. Negative thoughts and emotions are mental phenomena that occur as a consequence of depression. Some examples of negative thoughts and emotions are: "I am a failure", "I have no future", "I am worthless", "I am alone", "I have no way out", etc. These thoughts and emotions are normal and natural, but can be harmful if repressed or resisted. To accept your negative thoughts and emotions without fighting them, you can use the technique of radical acceptance, which consists of accepting what you feel and think without judging or avoiding it, but recognizing it as part of your experience.

Tip 5: Identify your personal values and commit to them. Personal values are principles or beliefs that guide the way we live and act. Personal values give us meaning and purpose to our lives, beyond external circumstances. Some examples of personal values are: honesty, generosity, justice, love, learning, etc. To identify your personal values, you can ask yourself questions such as: What is most important to me? What makes me proud? What makes me happy? What do I want to contribute to the world? To commit to your personal values, you can use the technique of active engagement, which consists of taking concrete, voluntary actions that are aligned with your values, without being driven by fear or guilt.

Tip 6: Set goals consistent with your values and take action to achieve them. Goals are specific and measurable objectives that we set out to achieve within a certain period of time. Goals help us orient our lives toward what we want and motivate us to take action to achieve them. However, not all goals are appropriate or beneficial for us. For a goal to be effective and healthy, it must meet the following characteristics: be specific, measurable, achievable, relevant and time-bound. For example, an appropriate goal would be: "I want to find a job that I like and that will allow me to make a decent living in the next six months". An inappropriate goal would be: "I want to be rich and famous someday". In addition to meeting these characteristics, goals should be consistent with your personal values, that is, they should reflect what you really want and care about in your life. To set goals that are consistent with your values, you can use the hierarchy of values technique, which consists of ordering your values according to their importance and priority for you, and then defining goals that relate to each of them. To take action to achieve your goals, you can use the action plan technique, which consists of breaking down your goals into smaller, more concrete steps, and assigning them a deadline and a person in charge.

Tip 7: Seek out activities that bring you satisfaction and well-being. Activities are actions we perform in our daily lives that allow us to take care of our basic needs, our obligations and our interests. Activities can be daily or pleasurable. Everyday activities are those that we have to do out of necessity or responsibility, such as eating, sleeping, grooming, working, studying, etc. Pleasurable activities are those that we do for pleasure or fun, such as reading, watching a movie, listening to music, practicing a hobby, etc. Both types of activities are important for our physical and mental well-being. Everyday activities help us to maintain a routine and order in our lives, to feel useful and productive, and to satisfy our basic needs. Pleasurable activities help us to enjoy the present, to feel happy and fulfilled, and to develop our capabilities and potential.

Tip 8: Take care of your physical and mental health. Health is the balance between body and mind. Physical health involves the proper functioning of the body's organs and systems. Mental health involves the proper functioning of cognitive, emotional and social processes. Physical and mental health influence each other, i.e. if one deteriorates, the other is also affected. Therefore, it is important to take care of both dimensions of health. To take care of your physical health, you can follow the following recommendations: eat a balanced and varied diet, drink enough water, avoid alcohol, tobacco and other drugs, do moderate and regular physical exercise, sleep 7 to 8 hours a day, maintain good personal hygiene, see a doctor when necessary, etc. To take care of your mental health, you can follow the following recommendations: practice relaxation or meditation techniques, avoid stress and anxiety, resolve conflicts peacefully, express your emotions appropriately, have a positive attitude towards life, seek emotional support when you need it, etc.

Tip 9: Learn to be flexible and adapt to change. Flexibility is the ability to adapt to changes and circumstances that arise in life. Flexibility implies accepting reality as it is, without denying or resisting it, but seeing it as an opportunity for learning and growth. Flexibility also implies being able to modify our plans or expectations when necessary, without clinging to them or becoming frustrated by them. Flexibility helps us to face problems with creativity and solvency, to take advantage of the opportunities offered to us, to tolerate uncertainty and risk, and to enjoy diversity and novelty.

Tip 10: Celebrate your accomplishments and recognize your strengths. Accomplishments are the positive results we get from performing an action or reaching a goal. Achievements help us to feel proud of ourselves, to value our effort and work, to improve our self-esteem and confidence, and to motivate us to keep moving forward. Achievements can be big or small, personal or collective, material or immaterial. The important thing is to recognize and celebrate them. To celebrate your achievements you can use the technique of positive reinforcement, which consists of rewarding yourself with something you like or that does you good every time you achieve an accomplishment. For example: if you find a job you like you can invite your partner to dinner; if you finish a course you are interested in you can buy a book you like; if you overcome a fear you can do something that amuses you, etc. These rewards can be material or immaterial, the important thing is that they make you feel good and that they recognize your merit.

Strengths are the capabilities or skills we have that enable us to face challenges and achieve our goals. Strengths help us to feel self-confident, to value our potential and talents, to improve our self-esteem and confidence, and to motivate us to keep learning and growing. Strengths can be of different types, such as intellectual, emotional, social, physical, etc. The important thing is to recognize them and develop them. To recognize your strengths you can use the strengths inventory technique, which consists of making a list of all the abilities or skills you have or would like to have, and then choose the ones you consider most important or relevant to you. To develop your strengths you can use the strengths training technique, which consists of practicing or improving the capabilities or skills you have chosen, through exercises, courses, books, etc.

Maria's case: how she overcame postpartum depression thanks to her family and therapist

Tip 1: Recognize that you have postpartum depression and need help. Postpartum depression is an illness that affects some women after giving birth. Postpartum depression is characterized by profound sadness, anxiety, insecurity, guilt, irritability, difficulty bonding with the baby, etc. Postpartum depression can have various causes, such as hormonal, biological, psychological, social or environmental factors, and can be treated with medication, psychotherapy or a combination of both.

Postpartum depression is not a weakness, guilt or shame, but a condition that can affect any woman. You can't fix it on your own, nor can you expect it to pass with time. You need to seek and accept professional and personal help to recover.

Tip 2: Seek professional help as soon as possible. Professional help is provided by doctors, psychologists, psychiatrists and other mental health specialists. These professionals can assess your situation, diagnose your postpartum depression, offer you pharmacological or psychotherapeutic treatment, and monitor your progress. Professional help is essential to treat postpartum depression effectively and safely.

Tip 3: Accept help from people who love you. Personal help comes from family, friends, colleagues and others who care about you and your baby. These people can offer you emotional, social and material support, listen to you, understand you, encourage you, accompany you, help you with daily chores and baby care, etc. Personal help is very important to feel accompanied, loved and supported.

Tip 4: Express your emotions appropriately. Emotions are psychophysiological reactions to certain stimuli or situations. Emotions can be positive or negative, depending on the degree of pleasure or displeasure they generate. Some negative emotions that are usually associated with postpartum depression are: sadness, anxiety, guilt, fear, irritability, etc. These emotions are normal and natural, but can be harmful if repressed or expressed inappropriately. To express your emotions appropriately, you can use the technique of emotional venting, which consists of releasing your emotions through words or actions that do not harm you or others. Some forms of emotional venting are: talking to someone you trust, writing a diary or letter, crying or shouting in a private place, doing physical exercise or an artistic activity, etc.

Tip 5: Strengthen your bond with your baby. Bonding is the emotional connection established between mother and baby from the moment of birth. Bonding is critical to the baby's physical, mental and social development and to the mother's emotional well-being. Bonding is created and strengthened through physical contact (skin to skin), gaze (eyes to eyes), voice (words to words), smell (nose to nose), taste (mouth to mouth) and hearing (sounds to sounds). To strengthen your bond with your baby, you can use the secure attachment technique, which consists of responding to your baby's signals (crying, smiling, gestures) in a sensitive and consistent way, offering security, trust and love.

Tip 6: Change your negative thoughts for positive ones. Negative thoughts are those that make you see reality in a distorted, exaggerated or irrational way, generating stress and anxiety. Some examples of negative thoughts are: "I'm not a good mother", "I don't love my baby", "I can't take care of my baby", "My baby doesn't love me", "This is horrible and there is no solution", etc. These thoughts are usually automatic, meaning that they appear without you realizing it, and repetitive, meaning that they repeat over and over again in your mind. To change your negative thoughts for positive ones, you can use the technique of positive internal dialogue, which consists of identifying these negative thoughts, evaluating their veracity and usefulness, and replacing them with positive thoughts that make you see reality in a more objective, realistic and constructive way. Some examples of positive thoughts are: "I am a good mother and I am doing the best I can", "I love my baby and he loves me", "I can take care of my baby with the help of others", "My baby is a gift and a blessing", "This is a challenge and I can overcome it", etc.

Tip 7: Value the positive aspects of your life. Positive aspects are the good things we have in our life that we can appreciate and be grateful for. Positive aspects can be big or small, personal or collective, material or immaterial. The important thing is to recognize and celebrate them. To appreciate the positive aspects of your life you can use the gratitude technique, which consists of making a list of all the things you are grateful for each day, and then expressing your gratitude verbally or in writing. Some examples of positive aspects for which you can feel gratitude are: your health, your family, your friends, your work, your home, your food, your clothes, your education, your culture, your nature, etc.

Tip 8: Enjoy the present and have hope for the future. The present is the moment in which we live and in which we can act. The future is the moment in which we project our desires and expectations. Both moments are important for our emotional well-being. The present helps us to enjoy what we have and do, to feel happy and fulfilled, and to develop our capabilities and potential. The future helps us to have enthusiasm and motivation for what we want and expect, to feel optimistic and confident, and to plan our actions and goals. To enjoy the present you can use the technique of mindfulness, which consists of paying attention to the here and now, without judging or being distracted by the past or the future. To have hope for the future you can use the technique of positive visualization, which consists of imagining in detail what your life will be like when you get what you want or expect.

Tip 9: Seek out activities that bring you satisfaction and well-being. Activities are actions we perform in our daily lives that allow us to take care of our basic needs, our obligations and our interests. Activities can be daily or pleasurable. Everyday activities are those that we have to do out of necessity or responsibility, such as eating, sleeping, grooming, working, studying, etc. Pleasurable activities are those that we do for pleasure or fun, such as reading, watching a movie, listening to music, practicing a hobby, etc. Both types of activities are important for our physical and mental well-being. Everyday activities help us to maintain a routine and order in our lives, to feel useful and productive, and to satisfy our basic needs. Pleasurable activities help us to enjoy the present, to feel happy and fulfilled, and to develop our capabilities and potential.

Tip 10: Strengthen your bonds with others. Attachments are the affective connections we establish with other people. Attachments help us to feel accompanied, loved and supported, to share our experiences, feelings and needs, to learn from others and to grow as people. Bonds can be of different types, such as family, friends, romantic, professional, etc. To strengthen your bonds with others, you can use the technique of effective communication, which consists of expressing your ideas, opinions and emotions in a clear, respectful and assertive way, actively listening to others, showing interest and empathy for what they say and feel, giving and receiving constructive feedback, resolving conflicts peacefully, etc.

8. Conclusion.

You have reached the end of this book, but not the end of your journey. You have learned a lot about depression, its causes, symptoms, treatments and solutions. You have discovered practical tools and useful tips that have helped you improve your physical and mental health, manage stress and anxiety, strengthen your self-esteem and optimism, and regain the joy of life.

But this book is not enough. This book is only a starting point, an impulse, a guide. The most important thing is what you do with what you have read. The most important thing is that you put into practice what you have learned, that you share what you have felt and celebrate what you have achieved. The most important thing is that you believe in yourself, in your abilities and in your dreams. The most important thing is that you live fully.

Depression can be overcome, but it is not easy or quick. It is a process that requires time, patience, effort and support. It is a process that has ups and downs, advances and setbacks, successes and failures. It is a process that involves changes, challenges, opportunities and learning. It is a process that transforms, strengthens, enriches and liberates you.

You are not alone in this process. You are not isolated or abandoned. There are many people who love you, support you and accompany you. There are many professionals who guide you, help you and treat you. There are many resources that inform you, motivate you and facilitate you. And there are many books like this one that offer you information, guidance and motivation to overcome depression.

I thank you for reading this wonderful book and for trusting me to help you with your project. I congratulate you for your courage, perseverance and determination to overcome depression and improve your quality of life. I admire you for your initiative, your creativity and your generosity in sharing your message of hope with others suffering from depression.

I wish you much success. I send you a virtual hug and a sincere applause. I encourage you to keep going, not to give up, not to get discouraged. I invite you to keep reading, to keep learning, to keep growing.

Soon we will upload more personal growth content so you can continue to enjoy reading and personal development. We are working to offer you the best self-improvement books to help you reach your goals and live happily.

Also by Santos Omar Medrano Chura

Aprende a escuchar las críticas. Cómo convertir los comentarios negativos en oportunidades de crecimiento.

La negación de lo desconocido. Cómo superar el miedo y la resistencia al cambio.

Learn to listen to criticism. How to turn negative comments into growth opportunities.

The denial of the unknown. How to overcome fear and resistance to change.

112 Consejos para fortalecer tu PACIENCIA y alcanzar tus metas

128 Consejos para el Mejoramiento Personal

Como ser un Buen Líder. Desarrolla el liderazgo para hacer una diferencia positiva en tu equipo y organización.

Desarrolla tu Inteligencia Emocional. Cómo entender y gestionar tus emociones para tener éxito en la vida.

Domina tu aprendizaje. Estrategias y técnicas efectivas para estudiar con éxito.

Elimina todo lo negativo de tu persona.

Aprendiendo a decir No sin sentir culpa o remordimiento. Cómo establecer límites saludables y tomar el control de tu vida.

El arte de la disciplina. Cómo lograr tus metas con hábitos saludables.

El mundo es tuyo. Cómo lograr tus sueños y vivir con plenitud.

El poder de la fuerza de voluntad. Cómo desarrollar hábitos positivos y alcanzar tus metas.

El secreto del ahora. Cómo vivir plenamente y sin estrés con la sabiduría del presente.

La mente resiliente. Cómo superar los obstáculos y los desafíos.

Mejoramiento del Cerebro. Cómo optimizar tu cerebro para una vida más plena.

Supera tu timidez.

Cómo anticiparse al futuro.

Como ser puntual. El arte de llegar a tiempo a todo.

El Poder de la Decisión. Desbloquea tu Potencial y Crea el Futuro que Deseas.

La Guía Definitiva para Criar Hijos Exitosos.

La mente ganadora. Cómo desarrollar el pensamiento de la gente exitosa.

La suerte no existe. Cómo crear tu propio destino con inteligencia y acción.

Mañana será otro día. Cómo afrontar los desafíos de la vida con optimismo.

Nunca Te Rindas 2. 76 consejos para alcanzar tus sueños sin rendirte.

Piensa como un triunfador. Los secretos de la psicología del éxito.

Vive la vida con optimismo.

Aléjate del hombre tóxico. Cómo liberarte de una relación destructiva y recuperar tu autoestima.

Al mal paso darle prisa.

Al mal tiempo, buena cara. Cómo encontrar la felicidad en las dificultades.

A palabras necias, oídos sordos.

Crisis Oportunidad. Cómo transformar los desafíos en éxitos.

Dime qué comes y te diré quién eres.

El poder de la positividad. Cómo rodearte de personas que te inspiran y te motivan.

El poder de las relaciones. Cómo elegir a las personas que te ayudan a crecer y a alcanzar tus metas.

El tiempo es oro. Cómo transformar tu vida con el poder del tiempo.

Gatitos felices. Todo lo que necesitas saber para cuidar a tu pequeño amigo.

Hazlo ya. Cómo dejar de procrastinar y cumplir tus sueños.

La luz al final del túnel. Cómo vencer la depresión y recuperar la alegría de vivir.

Libérate de la mujer tóxica. Cómo salir de una relación dañina y reconstruir tu felicidad.

No te culpes, actúa.

Pedalea hacia tus sueños. Cómo el ciclismo te ayuda a superar los obstáculos y alcanzar tus metas.

Planeta en peligro. Cómo proteger nuestro hogar común para las generaciones venideras.

Siempre listos. Cómo prepararse para cualquier situación y superar los desafíos de la vida.

Supera el miedo y abraza las oportunidades.

Tu sueño hecho realidad. Cómo transformar tu vida con el poder de tu mente.

Vencer al miedo. Estrategias prácticas para superar tus temores y alcanzar tus metas.

Vive en paz. Cómo sanar tu mente y tu corazón con la conciencia tranquila.

112 Tips to strengthen your patience and achieve your goals.

128 Tips for Personal Improvement. Set clear and achievable goals.

Develop Your Emotional Intelligence.

Eliminate everything negative about your person.

How to Be a Good Leader. Develop leadership to make a positive difference in your team and organization.

Master your learning. Effective strategies and techniques for successful study.

How to anticipate the future. Strategies and tips to be prepared for any situation.

Live life with optimism.

How to be punctual. The art of being on time for everything.

Overcome Fear and Embrace Opportunities.

There is no Such Thing as Luck.

Always ready. How to prepare for any situation and overcome life's challenges.

The Definitive Guide to Raising Successful Children.

The Power of Positivity.

Do It Now. How to Stop Procrastinating and Fulfill Your Dreams.

Don't Blame Yourself, Act.

Free Yourself from Toxic Women

Happy Kittens. Everything You Need to Know to Take Care of Your Little Friend.

Live in Peace. How to Heal Your Mind and Heart with a Clear Conscience.

Overcoming Fear. Practical Strategies for Overcoming Your Fears and Reaching Your Goals.

Planet in Danger. How to Protect Our Common Home for Generations to Come.

Stay Away from the Toxic Man.

The Light at the End of the Tunnel.

The Time Is Gold. How to transform your life with the power of time.

To Bad Weather, Good Face. How to Find Happiness in Difficulties.

To the Bad Step, Give Haste.

Your Dream Come True. How to Transform Your Life with the Power of Your Mind.

9 798223 637943